FAMOUS BLACK AMERICANS

FAMOUS BLACK AMERICANS

by **Morrie and Letha Turner**

JUDSON PRESS, Valley Forge

FAMOUS BLACK AMERICANS

Copyright © King Features Syndicate, Inc., 1973. World rights reserved. Republished from the **Black and White Coloring Book** by arrangement with Troubador Press, Incorporated.

All rights reserved. No part of this publication may be reproduced, stored in a retrieval system, or transmitted in any form or by any means, electronic, mechanical, photocopying, recording, or otherwise, without the prior permission of the copyright owner, except for brief quotations included in a review of the book.

Library of Congress Cataloging in Publication Data

Turner, Morrie.
  Famous Black Americans.

  CONTENTS: Crispus Attucks.—Benjamin Banneker.—Jean Baptiste Pointe de Sable.—Sojourner Truth. [etc.]
  1. Negroes—Biography. [1. Negroes—Biography]
I. Turner, Letha, joint author. II. Title.
[E185.96.T87]   301.45'19'6073 [B] [920]
ISBN 0-8170-0591-9

72-11224

Printed in the U.S.A.
JUDSON PRESS, Valley Forge, PA 19481

Contents

Crispus Attucks 6
Benjamin Banneker 14
Jean Baptiste Pointe De Sable 22
Sojourner Truth 30
Frederick A. Douglass 38
Ira Aldridge 46
Hiram Revels 54
Matthew A. Henson 62
William Edward Burghart Du Bois 70
Bill Pickett 78
George Washington Carver 86
Mary McLeod Bethune 94
Dr. Charles Drew 102
W. C. Handy 110
Langston Hughes 118

Crispus Attucks ? - 1770

Jean Baptiste Pointe De Sable 1745 - 1818

Frederick A. Douglass 1817 - 1895

Ira Aldridge 1805 - 1867

Hiram Revels 1822 - 1901

Matthew A. Henson 1867 - 1955

William Edward Burghart Du Bois 1868 - 1963

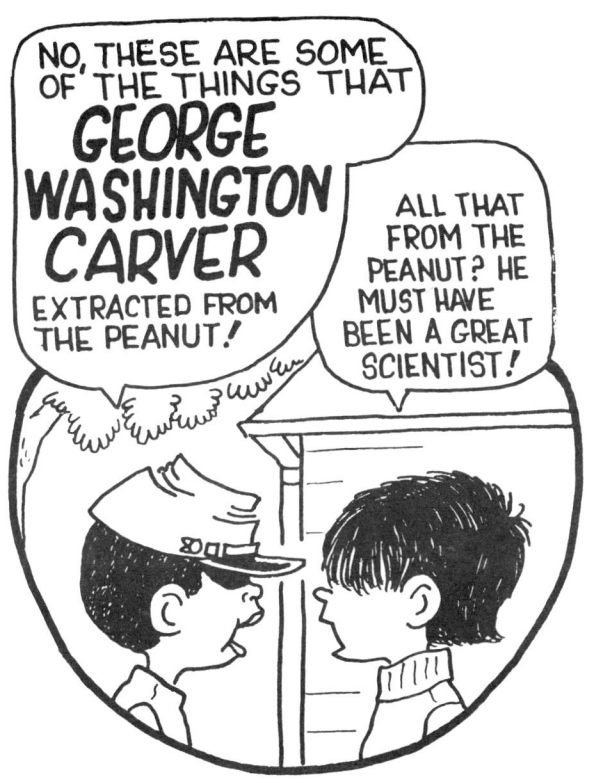

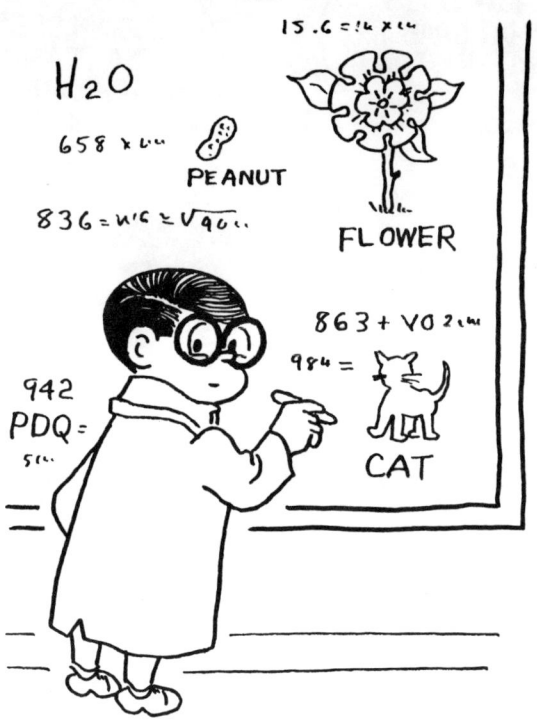

George Washington Carver 1864 - 1943

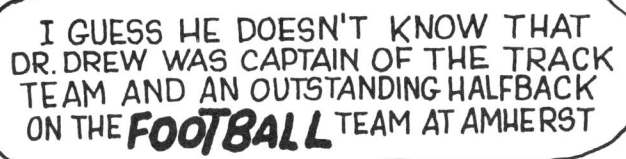

W. C. Handy 1873 - 1958

Langston Hughes 1902 - 1967